THE !

Mercury

Venus

Earth

Mars

Jupiter

Saturn

Uranus

Neptune

Pluto

Mercury

lattes and bears & things I can't remember or try to forget

I just ordered a grande coconut milk vanilla latte from the
Starbucks in Barnes & Noble. The barista asked me my name
with a decaffeinated smile on her face. I give it to her. Five minutes
and thirteen seconds pass, and she yells, *grande coconut milk vanilla latte
for Todd!* I approach the counter with espresso eyes. It's pointless to
correct her. So, I walked away.

I'm supposed to be writing a poem about memory & trauma &
blah, blah, blah, but I forgot or I don't remember or I don't want to
talk about it right now. I'm trying to forget.

I'm used to being called out of my name. Used to no one
remembering what I say. I wonder how Ty and Todd sound alike
or why I always seem to come here to write poems and people
watch. Dunkin' Donuts never gets my name wrong. Well, they
never ask. I'm glad they don't. That would ruin it.

I'm trying to forget or remember, then forget, I promise. I'm not
used to recalling something other than my name. This metaphor
may help: The bear caves in my chest. It tears into my limbs.

That would ruin it for me. Truth is, I would rather be called by a
name other than my own. I don't feel obligated to tell them I called
out of work and drove to Augusta to write this poem. I can lie
about my day and gloat about my life as a teacher, as a poet, as a
man, as Todd. She will forget him too.

It tears into my limbic system, multiplies & contorts, searches for
the soft spots it made last year. *Shhh,* I covered them with leaves &
I ache in places I'd rather not mention. I forgive you.

She will forget him tomorrow, so why does it matter if I lie or go to
Dunkin' Donuts. Their coffee doesn't make my stomach turn into a
cave of bubbles and bears and butterflies. My students know I
drink coffee when I'm having a bad day. I told the barista, whose
name I don't remember. She smiled for a tip.

I forgive you for reading this. I figured you would've stopped
by now. Did that metaphor work? You can call me Ty or Todd,
or victim, or virgin. I know you forgot my name too.

Mystery's skin can't heal / Mystery's skin can't heal / Mystery's skin can't heal / Mystery's skin can't heal / Mystery's skin can't heal / Mystery's skin can't heal / Mystery's skin can't heal / Mystery's skin can't heal / Mystery's skin can't heal / Mystery's skin can't heal / Mystery's skin can't heal / Mystery's skin can't heal / Mystery's skin can't heal /

the world refuses to read
the story of his Sunday bruises:
box springs swallow flesh
& shadows carve themselves into
someone else's lovely.

Watch & listen.

He is trying to tell you about the
wolves planted in crop circles,
but you only want to see the carpet.
He is trying to remember his name.

When August comes to abduct
Mystery's whisper of breathe &
nosebleeds, do not cover your ears,
& when the ring worms & blood
moons rise from his chest, trust your
eyes.

You will see the Trojan soldiers
drowning in his head & the memories
suffocating in his pillow.

& what it means to be a prisoner

of my own body: find me behind the apple tree in my throat picking switches

for switching too hard & breaking my back into bent wrists. I drown myself

in my own voice. ego is my cell mate. sleeps in my hollow bones & loves me.

I'm a no homo praise dance away from being saved, screaming my *man up*

like a hallelujah. *amen.*   *repent.*   *amen.*   *repent.*   *amen.* Til that masculine

spirit fills me up. I am a caged bird of prey pecking at scabs & the molting

feathers trying to escape my skin. *beat.*   *breathe. beat.*   *breathe.* Beat my wings

til the Walls of Jericho come crumbling down into a cradle. I am innocent. I am not dead, yet.

I do not need your guidance to return to   home or hell, but you call it the afterlife,

& I am comfortable in this straight jacket; I just need a pillow. The floor is frozen.

Venus

a love poem to gravity

you shadow of a man,
tell your gravity to deny my lips this verse. Drip the ink down my diaphragm.
I can't extract this unfamiliar melody without time to examine them.
I hide my words in your burial grounds of past lovers & decomposed love
letters to god, to man, to you. You abstract time & I limit this
this decaying flesh I wear to bed. I know these words are not footprints in your heart.
I could be a wave of passion growing stronger at the height of every full moon,
but I have grown weary of this world.

I would rather live with you on Venus, where it takes two
hundred & forty days to rotate on its axis, where there's
an unlimited access to love & time, where you & I
complement each other in ways unfamiliar to us
on Earth. Venus anoints my forehead with cocoa butter
kisses, finger paints stanzas down my body, smears emotions
across my chest, bathes me in her aphrodisiac upon her head,
each tightly coiled curl. The smell of black castor oil
leads me to an endless labyrinth of secrets
from the universe.

On Venus, I can open up this painted Pandora's box
in my chest & you can leave behind your carbon footprints.
I can diffuse every flaw, turn them inside out, fill *agape*
in my heart, lift this veil from my face, & prepare myself for you.

Tell your gravity to wean me off of your landscape. Pick me
from your cotton field. Hurry up & feed me to a Venus fly trap.
You wither rose petals. You vanish ice caps
You are the reason butterflies die.

I guess I will surrender my body to your circadian rhythm & dance
to your words I am unfamiliar with & do not have time to examine.

Cupid

You spent
your entire infancy

craving the love
you could not milk

from your
mother's breasts.

She looks down
& cries over what

used to be an ocean.
Opens her legs. Submerges

her fingers in an empty womb,
in search of the engagement ring

wrapped in your father's
infidelity.

You've spent
your entire adolescence

in closets hiding from
the love you couldn't leave

on your
mother's cheeks.

She reminisces over what used to be a ravine. Grieves over

what used to be a body.
Lifts her blouse in search

of the stretch marks left
by a lover.

Ty, don't you know they lead to you?

Pearls

Bite
the bullet
wound
in my neck
& swallow some liquid
pearls down your throat.

Scratch
those parts of your
palate
you never knew existed.
Feel the pinch
& the pain. Floss your teeth
with my skin.

There are places
on your body
you can not hide
from my hands.

Earth

where is the lady of the moon

light? She wants to guide you home.
She dances atop the water with her silk hair
rippling on the surface. She invites you
& the moths to cocoon in her screen door nightgown.

You better wait for the hymn to fall
from the mouth of the little bear in the forest.
When he winks at you, run from the cold
front porch. Listen to her whispers in the wind.

Can you see her quiver? Can you see her
pistol loaded bows & arrows in the sky?

Follow her fragrance underground.
Look! I'm waiting. Hurry! Hide in her
bonnet until the freedom of morning
comes to sweep you off of your feet.

Dance.

Let the underground railroad abolish you.

mama

It's the middle of August. The east winds start to roll in
& her children arrange a welcome mat out of eviction
notices to greet the friends they will only have til Mama's next payday.

Before the rent is due, they pack their bags, stack them behind
behind the front door to extend their stay without asking as
they tiptoe around a floor of broken windows.

Every morning, Mama calls the welfare office with food stamp
tears. Unable to provide for the children given to her by a God,
whose grace is sufficient, proficient in the art of blessings. They wonder,
"can the Lord lease his land to me"?

They've been locked out of a society exiled for their inability
to pull their Timberlands up to the American Dream. Their
possessions remain as permanent as the dew
forming in the backyard they do not own. You can't have a heart
without a home. So they wonder if this means they are heartless,
less of a human being?

Little did they know their mother was an alchemist by trade.
A prayer warrior who knocks down every pew in the way of
her blessing. Each hymn she sang turned their house into a
home & home into heaven. She would clasp her labored
hands
& turn those evictions into lullabies
her children fall asleep to every night
her prayers control the east winds
& turn those tears into a Baptist fit.

It's the end of August. The east winds are now a tornado.
The welcome mat is now
to another temporary home.
It's time for us to go.

martyrs watch the embers float

above this town tonight / a burning of haunted houses
& monsters / loading guns with prayers /
candlelit dinners turned date rape /
turned a day of remembrance /
a campfire ambushed by bodies /
of lye & kink / where will these embers rest /
where are those unmarked graves/
down the barrel / down the bottle

-in memory of black wall street

Mars

martians do not run away from fires

& their hooves do not sink / in quicksand /
they hover above the streets /
with the rapture / in their hands /
church steeples mixed with charred bones /

-in memory of little Africa

I've been shot

I've been shot
by a man I've never met.

He put his pistol to my chest
bringing back flashes of blue & red lights
I've seen before.

As I fell on the concrete floor,
I tried looking passed his shades
to get a glimpse of his soul,
but the sole of his shoe
was forced into my holy temple.

He wrapped his injustice around my
wrists,
his hatred around my neck,
& stripped my identity
from my back pocket.

He's never met me before
but he's seen my face
countless times on the TV screen.
He drives by my house waiting to see
if I would reach for the stereotype
he's placed in front of me.

He's seen my nappy-headed hair
on the front of magazines.
He's seen my brown eyes
downsized by hate crimes & white
privilege.
I'm forced to compromise.

You see we've known each other
for quite some time,
but this time I cried
as I laid in a pool of my blood & black
pride.

Momma warned me this day might come:

"Keep your hands on the wheel, son."
"Stay calm and respect the officer, son."
"Do everything he tells you to do, son."

Momma, I did everything you said to do:
"Officer, I can't breathe."
"Officer, my hands are up."
"Officer, I have a family to feed."

But he shot me.
My body naturally resisted,
this expected occurrence of my black
existence.

It is now (insert date & time).
I have finally become
an official victim of a global genocide.
This nation will continue to divide
until you find meaning in my life & my death.

I've been shot
by a man I've never met
& I finally figured out
what it means to be
a Black man in America.

17

You dropped a bomb on me

baby. you called
& said
it was buried
in my
       chest

You lit the fuse, I stand accused

near the bed
where you last
laid your hands
on me
       question:

I won't forget what you done

who
did you
forget first? me
or the
       bomb?

Jupiter

Cupid

When your father was young, your grandmother knew
I would not be around for long. She kept my name

& I took away his wings & gave them to the sky.
He's been waging a war against me ever since.

I was never there to wipe the fire from his eyes &
I turned my back on his anger. His blood

shed into the night & made it day
& not even time could wash it away.

When you were younger, you tried flying
higher than the arrows he gave you.

The sun burned your plastic wings & they melted.
Can I take the pain away for a little while

or kiss your burnt, dead skin? Don't bother him
with your darts of dandelion seeds.

Ty, don't you know they lead you.

Father Figure

Behind these man-made
prison cells you know
him: a man made of original sin,
genetically coded with
DNA from a ghost
who sings you lullabies
with his sentences.
You are familiar with his
poorly written syntaxes
written on taxpayer dollars,
but you never learned
how to say *daddy*.
I don't blame you
because you never had
a reason to.

-     signed your father,
      whose brown eyes you've never
      been lost in.

Behind each misspelled word
& watermarked photograph,
you will paint a picture &
give this ghost new life.
Every capitalized word
will be your form of
discipline.
Every punctuation will
stop your back talking
in its tracks.
Every new sentence,
every missing *I love you*,
will leave you to wonder.

-     signed your father,
      whose arm hairs have never
      been plucked by your curiosity.

Behind time lies a
teenage boy who tries
finding synonyms for love
He will create a baseball
out of each letter & throw
Them in a fireplace
as a metaphorical expression
he feels the periods puncturing
his imagination each comma
splice burns the bridge he's
spent a lifetime creating.
Anticipation will become
hesitation & then
frustration will turn into
condemnation will turn into
the cremation of a young
boys heart.

- signed your father,
whose cheap cologne
scent will never
trigger memories.

Behind your innocent
5-year old smile
lies a prayer waiting
to be released
read between the lines
signed your father,
whose voice has
grown stronger
with each letter.

- signed your father,
whose voice has grown
stronger with each letter.

Bodies

your hand
is the same
color as the air
floating
above
my throat.

do you feel
obligated
to grab
bodies
too ripe
for death

to give
them back
to the land
from which you
stripped them
from?

Saturn

mAss

I remembered Annie walking into the room
upstairs. You were mixing your semen with
my vomit in the toilet bowl.
My head cracked on the tiles like a crystal
ball. She mistakes this as consensual.
She must have thought the distance
between you & I was foreplay,
& my fetal position was a magic trick.

I remember the way you tried to comfort
me downstairs. Your hand suffocated mine.
You broke my dry bones with a whisper &
a death blow on my cheek. You stole my
voice without asking.

Why did you kiss these trembling lips when
they could break at any moment?
Why did you try hold these hands when
they've been struggling with the weight of
their own?

I remember. Your lips are heavy in this
sanctuary. Your hands give me splinters on
this altar. You changed the face of God.
Made them into a pillow or a cum rag.
I can't remember.

Monochrome rainbow

Somewhere over the monochrome rainbow,
black birds fly by my peripheral,
visions of a Technicolor nightmare fades to black.

A black father's love fades into anger.
A black father's pride fades into shame.
A black father's son fades into a faggot.

Tonight,
a black father will purchase a straight
jacket: comfort & convert his only
son through victimizing conversations,
suicidal proclamations & refrains of
you are all I have.

Here comes the interlude: stripped
away all of his hues. Left him
an empty black body
waiting to be placed
into a body bag.

Suffocating in paragraphs of biblical verses,
the black father is unsure of how to use
but abuse, abuse was on the tip of his tongue,
ready to be emptied & reloaded
until his black son was straightened out.

Forced the son into a horizon of yellow
brick roads & signs of the sinner's
prayer & pitchforks & tin men
without hearts they could bear on the sleeve
of a condom. No top or bottom,
no fairy Godmother, no shooting star,
no man behind the mirror could ever
love a son the way a father could.

Daddy, you took away all of my sunshine.

Let me pray this gay away, daddy.

Let me bruise my knees
for anything other than sexual advances.

Let me concoct a mixture of holy water & bleach
& digest *your* sanctity, *your* holy, *your* blessed assurance.

Let me change this faggot into a man,
this bundle of sticks into a forest fire.
Let me hold you tighter than homophobia.

Please stay my father, always.

Let me click these heels of red
cause there's no place like home.

My only wish – for you to love my queer,
the dearest deepest part of me. I dare
hide behind my black curtain of a skin.
You be my kin,
but don't you see I'm tired
of walking, daddy.

My best friend, who you thought
I'd fall in love with--
I'll never fall in love with her. Daddy,

Dance with me. Before your winter
solstice steals my sunshine. Daddy,
sorry I'm a nuisance.

Somewhere over the rainbow,
I speak in this monotone phoning home,
waving a white flag, a false deliverance.
I see bluebirds fly.

Daddy, you can't stop my sunshine.

But I will love my me,

my queer,
 my black.

& Daddy,

I love you.

Avril Lavigne's "Complicated" plays at AFROPUNK FEST Atlanta & everyone sings along & this is what it means to be black

& this is what it means to love. You hold my hands & kiss
them for the first time without conviction. *Is my hand suppose to*

cover yours or vice versa? I hold your breathe while you stand in
line, ordering us the blackest chicken & waffles I've ever

tasted. You come back & it's hidden & you can't find it &
maybe you forgot to ask because you know I'll keep it safe.

This is radically beautiful & alternative. We sing together &
love with an echo & a silence & *You become somebody else /*

*'round everyone else / watching your back, like you can't relax / You're
trying to be cool, you look like a fool to me.* I use to sing this

song like a sin at the bus stop on the iPod I stole & hid it in
the closet among other things. I kept the volume low &

when someone looked my way, I turned blacker and bluer &
hid my shadow under the moon. *And you fall and you*

crawl and you break / And you take what you get and you turn it into honesty.
This is the case for everyone here: radically beautiful &

alternative. We continue singing & loving our black & blue
bodies under the moon, I*s my hand suppose to cover yours or vice*

versa? & this is what love feels like & to love & to be loved.

Uranus

monarch

i.

at birth larvae, wide-eyed & bewildered,
inspect every blade of grass & circle
around the roses & amuse themselves
on the leaves of milkweeds. there they
practice yoga & taking breaks to destroy
their elevated bungalows,
meditating, preparing for their
rite of passage without their nectarous
conventions they enter a chrysalis

ii.

in the chrysalis they die to themselves
they beat on their crystallized cocoon
like a heart thump thump it breaks
they erupt into peace sleepwalking angels
with no vertebrate linger in the breeze
bathe in new light become a fragment of
a kaleidoscope the world is not prepared for
to reveal a soon-to-be augmented beauty

iii.

in their final form, they exit this crowded place,
inhaling nostalgia & exhaling wanderlust.
they allow heaven's holy breeze to
travel through the spiracles in their thorax &
swallow a molted skin, imagining the colors
humans are unable to see.
They migrate to the gateways of Alebeline
where they are crowned & continue
to digest the milkweeds, they store
the poison of the world. one final stretch.
their wings to the sun & fly
unabashedly they become.

boys with the sweet grass roses

This is a poem about black boys, no older than
thirteen, made of polyester carpet
burns made tender by granny & auntie's kisses.
His twists & cornrows fade & his lined up
waves sink the sea islands.

They be escaping Columbus & making his way
through America. They be squeezing through
society & staring Calhoun in his stone eyes.
They be meeting ghosts at the south end of
market with the other black boys.
They become friends.

Why do people cross the road when they see
them? Why don't people stop for the
sweet grass they smelling? Watch this rose
bloom. Chew the sun flower seeds.
Catch them in the tortoise shell.

struggle is an ex lover

who I'm still in love with.
Stronger than when
          we met in 1863,
more passion than
          I've seen since we eloped
last Juneteenth to escape that
          quiet, slow-moving town
in Maycomb county,
          where I could hear his heart

beat. He loves me

          enough to display his sovereignty.
He makes me moan & scream
          beneath his white sheets. Most mornings
my mind makes me believe
          I was nothing without his stainless steel fingers
wrapped, interlocked
          around my wrists. I was born to dye
his white collar garments black & blue
          from in between his legs. I became a wet rag
waiting to be wrung out til old wine drips

from my lips. He loves me

          enough to splatter black walls & concrete streets
with the smell of a familiar fire. Before the sun sets
          behind us, they collapse without me in the distance.
I can hear mockingbirds flying between
          the nuance of dusk & dawn. My eyes squint
to assure myself they won't be killed.
          He makes my heart melt the way ice
cubes melt in Carolina Sweet Tea &
          forces my legs around him the way heat
wraps its legs around asphalt driveways

mid- August. He says *I love you,*

Enough! So, I close my mouth & do what he says.

Struggle is an ex lover,
        who will never give me closure.
Centuries have passed since
        our honeymoon, yet I still hear
Jim crows singing & nightingales traveling
        beneath the north star. I still smell his cufflinks
dabbed in a cologne of nylon.
        How could I say no to a man whose firm
hands condition my African roots
        & cripple me? I fall for him each time

I try to run away. I thought he loved me.

        Each Sunday I wake to the same bouquet of sweet
grass roses he said he made for me.
        Day in, day out he forces his fragrance
around my steam pressed blue collar.
        He became my one nation under
God & my insecurity became his
        fetish as he serenaded me
beneath an orange sky
        of freshly burnt love letters synonyms for suicide
notes. Till this day he writes me every Valentine's,

        he says, *I love you*, as a catalyst to my relapse.

Struggle is an ex lover,
        who envies my lust for Freedom.
I want him to touch me all over
        & give me a taste of a newer wine.
Freedom, I can see you in the
        distance teasing me with your salvation.
I want you more than ever.
        Why are you hiding from me?
Freedom, sweep me off of my feet. I want you
        to fill my ears with your fantasies.

Freedom, I will make you love me.

Watch as I peel these layers of silk
from around my hardened
heart. I don't mind contorting my body
to be exactly what you want it to be.
Let me lift every voice
& sing to you. Freedom,
you can be my National Anthem & I will place
my hand upon my heart because it is yours.
Freedom, I dream of you every night. I think of you
every time Struggle forces himself onto me.

I love you. So, why don't you want me?

Neptune

drowning

when people think
you are lying
tell them
your body
can (not)
hold their burdens

i can't breathe

the guilt
of the Atlantic
trickles into
a trembling cave
drowning
the beast
in your belly

i can't breathe

tell them
you are (not)
a story teller
your story
teaches them
how to keep a horse
from drinking water

i can't breathe

reach for the air
they have stolen
& kept
as a souvenir
squeeze the glass
from their throats
burn the message
from their second
voyage

i can't breathe

they have tried
taking away
your language
of gravity
turning typhoons
into sea foam
drown them
they deserve it
how else will
they learn to swim

they can't breathe

To the lionfish:

You & me
have something
in common:

displaced

disjointed

kidnapped from our Mother's uterus
ships became our home

our bodies ferment
in a crowded oak barrel

our new lives in
the hands of a system

our misery made
into a delicacy

then they wonder why
we're angry

our color

a warning

do not let
our spines
fool you

the myth of winter

Convince him
    to drink an avalanche of alcohol &
      wait til he chokes,
        then drag him

the peak to the mountain
    & hope he forgets.
      The snow-painted
        mile markers
lead him to the futon
    by the fireplace
      underneath
        the wilted mistletoes.
Whisper hot chocolate
    to the hibernating bear.
      Start a campfire
        with his Jesus jeans.
Turn up the volume
    on the record player.
      Holy night,
        Place a fresh scent
of snow over his body
    All is calm
      & place his head
        on the pillow.
Taste the innocence
    Round yon Virgin
      melt down a river
        & suffocate him
in evergreen leaves
    to cover your bourbon
      tracks on his body.
        Kiss him.
Expose his body
    to Pneumonia
      & tell him he liked it.
Text him
    an apology.
      It's the only way
        you can move
to the next season.

Pluto

it became autumn

You wake up
the next morning
to an atonement
you quickly dismiss

& throw your phone
down in frustration
because sex
was the last thing

on your mind.
All is calm
You begin to think
if you had stayed

in your dorm room studying
would you have the scars
Shepherds quake at the sight
to prove *you* are still *you*?

You hold on to that apology
as tight as melting
ice & let your body
be a reminder of evergreens.

Carve blame
into your shoulder
like the snow angel
you made under the mistletoe.

Lather,
rinse,
& repeat the memories.

Try your best
to wash them out.
Scratch your scalp.
Wonder if it really happened.

Peel back
the scars. Dwell
in the dark
for a little while.

Forgive him.
Holy Night
It's the only way
you will be able to

appreciate winter again.

41

On my father's birthday,

he lectured me about heartbreak. I
wanted so badly to telepathically
communicate to him about ██ &
how I loved him.

I reassured him my chest was full &
didn't say much (except those phrases
children use to rush their parents off
of the phone). I wish I could. I'm not
sure what would hurt the most:
the thought of my father sending me
back to space or the space ██ could
leave behind.

I grew wings from my neck & hung
myself from the moon to see how
long I could hold my breath.
I swallowed the Northern Lights &
tried to birth a black hole, but my
body couldn't handle churning the
Milky Way anymore.

My knees submitted to gravity that
night & I threw my sins under God's
finger nail, waiting to see if He was
really alive. He never answered, but I
found heartbreak dancing in the belly
of a whale. ██ should be having
the time of his life without me.

One day, on my father's birthday, I
will talk to him about heartbreak & I
will not be scared of space.

self-care portrait

finger painting   is simple   it is an art   I take much
                              pride in   the simple act
                    of caressing the body   of a stretched canvas   with your
                              fingers   dancing

      between the freedom   of acrylic   the way my index   & ring finger
                                                     fall slowly
into an abyss   of nothingness   amazes me   each time
                              each time paint kisses

      the canvas   I feel like   the alpha   & omega
                                    i feel confident invading
white spaces   these mistakes   are transformed   into a
                              collection   masterpieces.

now close your eyes   you have nothing to prove   to the world
                                                          celebrate
each pigmentation   each blackhead   & blemish   taste
                              the graffiti   on your lips

      picture colors   you will never   be be able to replicate
                                             the world watches
      as your color   drips from your fingertips   become who you
                                    were meant to be

            you are the true alchemist   magic   is at the disposal   of your
                                                          fingertips
            transform trauma   allow your bliss   to arise   from each
                                    cuticle   tear apart

      the context   stretch the canvas   use both hands   & open your
                              eyes   for the world to see
                                    practice the art   of the moment

ACKNOWLEDGMENT

Versions of *Struggle is an ex lover, Drowning,* and *the myth of winter* have appeared in For The Scribes and the inaugural issue of The Good Juju Review. I would like to thank both publishers for believing in the work of a little black boy like me.

Writing this book forced me to decide the kind of writer I wanted to be. Thanks to Matthew Foley and Derek Berry of Contribute your Verse for coaching me and pushing me beyond my creative limits, Marcus Amaker for being a mentor, Saeed Jones for his brotherhood and always one upping me in Poetry Slams, and Yasmeen Sayyah for our hookah dates and love for poetry.

Thank you Ja'lessa, Alexus, and Vanity for all the shade and love you throw my way.

Thank you Will for letting me know it's okay to be vulnerable

A special thank you to my uncle, Erle, for being an unexpected hero, Mrs. Heard, for believing in her *mijo*, and Brooke, for making this dream come true.

Without the support of my friends, family, and fellow poets and believers, this book would still be a dream.

Made in the USA
Columbia, SC
03 October 2018